PENGUIN BOOKS
AND . . . PERHAPS LOVE

Sanil Sachar is a national best-selling author from India, traversing through prose, poetry, short-stories, scripts and couplets that have been critically acclaimed and received by readers around the world. With over 200 works of poetry and short stories, Sachar is one of the few Indian authors to be published in all forms of literature.

His work in the world of business also includes him founding an incubator in New Delhi, India, by the name of Huddle, which has incubated leading sector agnostic start-ups in the consumer, blockchain, electric vehicle and health sectors, to name a few. An avid sportsperson, Sanil Sachar is also one of the co-owners of the global sports brand Tru, whose flagship innovation and product, Trusox, high-technology performance socks, are worn across nine sports and across the globe.

A highly acclaimed columnist, a triple TED Speaker who has addressed international audiences on a number of leadership aspects, apart from on innovation through creativity with the likes of Google, JCB, TCS and Wipro, Sachar is an artist and innovator with a passion to drive change, one word at a time.

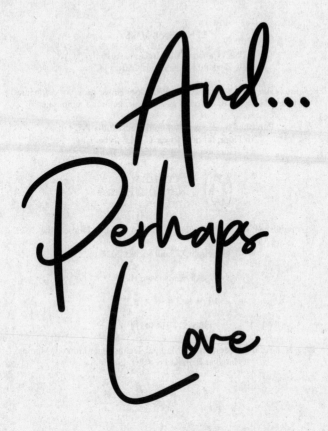

And... Perhaps Love

SANIL SACHAR

PENGUIN BOOKS

An imprint of Penguin Random House

PENGUIN BOOKS

USA | Canada | UK | Ireland | Australia
New Zealand | India | South Africa | China

Penguin Books is part of the Penguin Random House group of companies
whose addresses can be found at global.penguinrandomhouse.com

Published by Penguin Random House India Pvt. Ltd
7th Floor, Infinity Tower C, DLF Cyber City,
Gurgaon 122 002, Haryana, India

Penguin
Random House
India

First published in Penguin Books by Penguin Random House India 2020

Copyright © Sanil Sachar 2020

10 9 8 7 6 5 4 3 2 1

ISBN 9780143451198

Typeset in Adobe Caslon Pro by Manipal Technologies Limited, Manipal
Printed at Replika Press Pvt. Ltd, India

www.penguin.co.in

Love has the power to bring together, and occasionally it is love that uses its might to cause a break. Like a pendulum, it dictates how our time will be spent and like oxygen it is the reason we live. Without oxygen, we see no light and without love, well, there is no life.

Contents

Contents

DEMOLITION

EXPLORATION

RECOVERY

AWAKENING

From the Author . . .

Now that I've your attention, here's the bitter truth. You will succeed. You will fail. You will love. You will hate. But the bright side of this is: You will continue to do everything. This is life and that is the bitter truth.

On the Scheme of the Book

Each section in this book has a theme. Every page has a voice for every mood that shapes life. Turn to this book whenever you need someone to speak to. Turn to it whenever you want to be heard. Mostly, turn to it with no expectation because only then will it leave you with something you didn't know you have.

As you'll discover, none of the words are labelled with a subject. Simply because labels are fixed, leaving no room to breathe, amidst these dialogues, every word has its own freedom. It is for you to determine when to label them, what to label them and if you wish to label them.

And ... Perhaps Love is everything you've experienced and everything you will experience.

Each turn of the page is a new chapter and an instance of life as you've encountered.

On the Scheme of the book

Introduction

Spaces. A finite word with an infinite connotation. It lingers at the beginning and end of everything we do. Before you set yourself on a path, there is a space between where you are and where you're going to be. Before you know it, who you are is almost always who you were a moment ago. The space in between is the reflection of when your past and future meet; some call it the present.

Spaces. They demand nothing but fluidity. A sense of freedom that we almost instantly lose as we do something for the first time and fill up the space of ambiguity with what becomes a benchmark to either meet or surpass. Fill up the space and the innocence is lost. But why can't we create spaces?

Spaces. Remind me of the comfort of a pillow. Almost like a friend who is there to save me from trouble or help me create it. There is a feeling of foreverness in its imagery, making anyone seem like a hopeless wanderer, and a hopeful arriver.

Spaces. Found in between these pages that words couldn't find. The conceptualization of this book mirrors how we all live. There are words linked to one another, with spaces filled from the first page to the end. We've all been through a time where we know too little and then we know too much. This stands true for everyone in the world, but there is an age when we are in-between, and when we reach on the other side, we wish to unlearn, and learn again. This bridge is best defined by the spaces. The home of unspoken words.

Spaces. They don't follow any norm, any agenda or any fixed method, yet they find their way. So, forget what you know of books, and find yourself in these filled and unfilled spaces because no one else will ever see how you see your reflection, and that's what makes your space yours.

This is not a book written by someone, as much as it is a biography of *you*, today, whichever 'today' *you* pick this up on. Wherever *you* begin, and wherever *you* want to leave it, there are blank pages speaking to *you*, for *you* to speak back. This book is not written just for *you* to read; there's more it stands for. It stands to stand by *you*, and demands *you* speak back. Promoting vulnerability as a sign of strength, and the first step of letting go, in order to consume what awaits *you*.

If there is one certainty, it lies in the fluctuation of every second, within each and every human, that causes the uncertainty of their emotions. Before you acknowledge what you are feeling, it passes, and before you pre-empt what will happen, you are there. This buffet of life and variety are what constitutes the core of the book. A moment, not of realization, but of acknowledgement.

While a human being is best described as being in a state of confusion, this book speaks to the lovers finding love, in a human, in an object, in an action, in a moment, in the future, and hopefully at all times, in themselves. This is an experimental book, constructed to help you experiment. It acts as a silent observer for when you want to read it, and a silent listener when you want to communicate to it.

This is not a book written to be read from start to finish. There is no order in which each of us emotes. Therefore, being unorganized is not chaos, it is a way of life. The conceptualization of this book mirrors how we all live. There are words linked to one another, from the first page to the end. Then, there are separate pages that act as a mirror reflecting who you feel you are today. Emotions, actions, thoughts, all these are a reflection of themes, which make up a physical being. Therefore, there are themes that rest within, providing a flavour and pick of the day, depending on where *you* are today. Or simply picking it up to lose yourself in a part *you* wish *you* were today.

MUSE

(i)

The Beginning of the End

I could pick any spot in the world and I picked her smile to be my happiness, forgetting that her smile was not dependent on my happiness.

~

The beauty of being in love with someone is that you get to live your life and theirs and it's often rare to be able to live two lives at once and that's what makes love, life.

~

We met unexpectedly. Fell in love unexpectedly. Fought, made up, went up and down, like seesaws our lives fluctuated in tempo but we stuck together because that's where we found our comfort.

~

Silence speaks louder,
As the proximity decreases,
Words feel heavier,
As they stay locked in your cages.

Darkness feels brighter,
To an intoxicated mind,
Deluded, it wanders,
What can't be held,
Should not be a mission to find.

I speak to you through words you don't see,
You say what you have to,
Just not to me,
Ecstasy, this distance,
Which teases a conversation yet to brew,
You sip on your comfort,
I slowly sip mine,
This comfortable silence is nirvana,
Gifted to me, by you.

~

*The pianist in the background serenaded us, adding a theme to our first-time conversation which could very well be our first and only dialogue. Only time would tell.

From glaring lights making it easier to read, to scribbled thoughts, the beams dimmed, setting a tone of comfort between two strangers.

She stood up, and in that moment, I realized I didn't want her to leave. Holding my words within before I could ask her to stay, she offered me a pencil-thin cigarette, which resembled her lipstick-shaped fingers. I couldn't refuse, accepting her offer only to realize I don't smoke, but then again neither do I have strange encounters.

Standing in a glass cubicle, smoke enveloped what became a more comfortable setting. Maybe it was the whisky in me which enabled me to stay calm and fearless in the silence that stood between us as my mind rehearsed what to say next. The cigarette continued to burn closer to my fingers, unsmoked; I played along with the burning stick, pretending to be more lost in the conversation than I was just so I can forget to inhale.

Sanil Sachar

As she continued to ash, a third stranger waved from the other side of the window. He turned out to be a stranger for one and a familiar, much-anticipated significant for the other.

While I thought the cigarette was a filler for the time between our pauses, I turned out to be the filler as she waved good riddance and hello in the same motion, leaving me alone in a smoked-filled box.

Right then I learned even a filler can have its own filler, as I experienced my first encounter inhaling a cigarette, reiterating that these burning sticks lead to no good.

*Flashback

~

Look at us,
A one-night drink?
A one-night song?
A melody that sticks,
A rhythm that ticks memories that went too fast,
That passed too soon.

Look at us,
A one-night drink?
Maybe one-two more,
Maybe one more bottle?
Or an endless tap,
There's more to this,
Let's figure with time,
Let's study with wine.

There's more to this,
I evaluate your tricks,
Studying me like something you know,
Inspecting me like a moment to let go,
Is this a one-night drink?
Is this a moment we'll let sink?

How about we drink to know?
And wander from the word go,
Tread from the times we speak of,

Learn about what we do,
Without having to conceal,
What we don't know,
What we don't see,
That which will learn when we unveil,
So how about that one drink?

~

And . . . Perhaps Love

She came to me and told me we'd see the world,
Intoxicated, like a globe our head swirled,
We saw the world and a few more stars,
Infatuated, we grew into this deeper, intertwined, curled.

She leaned forward and I leaned in too,
She moved back and realized I'm a whisper away,
From strangers to lovers, never calculating how our
time flew,
We brisked through the ages of yesterday,
All my energy, all our love,
Restored and rejuvenated before they turned to dust,
In a duffle bag labelling me a hippie,
Confused and excited of what is yet to be,
She leaned in and gave me a map,

With a hole through which I saw her,
She told me we'll see the whole world too,
A universe constructed from our definitions,
No destinations,

I'm intrigued, a balloon of exhilaration,
She came to me and I don't question no more,
What will be will be, we're all first-timers,
Inexperienced, impatiently waiting to explore.

(ii)

Trigger Point

'Do you want to get a cup of coffee sometime?'

'Not if you're going to be this vague about it,' her response was unmasked without a pause.

'Fine, do you want to get a cup of iced latte sometime?'

My reply earned a laugh she was holding back. Her smile creating dimples she couldn't hide, the moment her mind hugged happiness.

'Sometime could mean a year from now too, how about we get this latte then?' Each word that left her mouth reminding me I needed to pick my words wisely.

'Sometime could be now as well.'

'Then why didn't you say it?'

'Because I wasn't sure you'd say yes now.'

'Then what makes you sure I'll say yes later.'

'Nothing. But I'll be able to build the courage to face rejection then.'

'You're scared of being rejected?'

'Generally, in life, no. By you, yes.' I was surprising myself with the conversation that flowed unfiltered.

She looked at her watch, the seconds hand moved yet time appeared to be on a standstill. The adrenaline from the moment did the job the coffee would, as anxiety set its own benchmark.

'Sometime has begun.' She looked up at my nervous expression. The look on her was the opposite, balancing the moment.

~

She was an incredible orator, as the most mundane words seemed like the work of a wordsmith. I knew nothing about her but for the fact she could be a magician hypnotizing me with each syllable. All she asked me was one question and I found myself dumbstruck figuring out an answer that would lead us into a conversation. But she had something else in mind, and it would be a while till I would figure what part I played.

(iii)

Chemical Reaction

I sit here wondering how these sessions would be of any help. This isn't my first session and I know I don't have the courage for it be my last. Listening to buzz words that excite any exhausted body, sting my ears in the form of distant and unrealistic dreams. Another weekend spent searching for the answers. Sitting next to me, she writes into a nimble, overcrowded notepad. None of the words preached are reflected on her notes.

'Not being able to get any answers you want either, do you?' I muster up the courage and whisper, like a student scared of being caught in class. 'I'm not here to find answers.' Her eyes focused on the remaining gaps yet to be inked on her paper. I wonder why she would show up knowing there was nothing to be offered. Just then, almost like my thoughts were sprayed on her notepad, she passed me a note with a bold sentence, *'Sometimes, when you are looking for the path, you should make an effort to get lost in the process.'*

(iv)

Inflection

Love is the only element powerful enough where the pain is worth taking. Where the pain makes you happy because it showcases your vulnerability and strength to face weakness. The same way you don't anticipate the striking of love, the transformation it brings in you is as big a surprise.

~

Her eyes read through mine,
That are heavier as I float into a new canvas,
Paddling through clouds,
Parched and impatient to where we are bound.

~

She takes a picture of him as he learns to smile again. His face pressuring each muscle, creating crevices that will define an expression of undisputed contentment.

He looks at her, smiling. She is the first reason for his missing smile, and her eyes hidden behind the camera fill up with tears.

He is the reason for the sweetest tears she will shed.

~

Her smile was innocent, almost like she didn't know
how to do it.

A face that spoke more through the crevices around
the mouth than the mouth itself. She was ambiguous
without intending to be. You couldn't fall anything but
in love with her, and he was slowly realizing that he
couldn't wait for it to happen any quicker to him.

~

We looked at each other as if we were the only two people in the world. As though, nothing else around us was real, except the abnormality of the intensity which grew unparalleled.

(v)

Conviction

Love is the most powerful tool we have. It's even more
powerful when it's not in the hand of the warrior,
fighting to earn love.

Love has the power to bring together, and occasionally
it is love that uses its might to break. Like a pendulum,
it dictates how our time will be spent, and like oxygen,
it is the reason we live. Without oxygen, we see no light
and without love, well, there is no life.

~

She sat there sipping her tea while I sipped the cinnamon-scented coffee that gave an instantaneous kick. It wasn't the caffeine that played this part but her crooked smile that emerged evenly from both sides of her lips. I'd seen this smile before but unlike the coffee, I could never get immune to the reflexive shiver it left within . . . like the drop of cold water down your back, it was a chill that ended with a warmth within.

~

And . . . Perhaps Love

Write me a song,
As I close my eyes and watch the hours, long,
That walk slowly,
Creeping on us,
Write me a song,
And gift me these times.

Tell me what's wrong,
And show me how to make it right,
Let the trouble we don't plan,
Be an adventure,
One where you are the reason for my right.

Serenade me with your whisper,
As they envelope me in lonesome days;
Embrace me with your smile,
The one, where my heart doesn't mind when it breaks.

~

Take me, take me to the depth of the summer,
Where time melts in the embraces of forever,

Carry me, as I carry you into the wilderness,
Let's share this fear, let's share our mess,

Study me, until I become the student,
Measuring each crevice,
Identifying my definition of finesse,

These drunken days don't stand a chance against
tomorrow,
As they wash away in hazy nights,
Forgetting yesterday's sorrow,

So, fall first, fall fast,
Start now, stop last,
As, in today's sun we continue to bask,
In the shade of our times,
Where we play artist and observer,
Sometimes student and teacher,
Forever sinner, seldom the preacher.

(vi)

Love and Its Allies

There are two kinds of people in this world. Lovers
educated about love from the love they get, and lovers
transformed from the love they have lost. I am an object
of the love that was not reciprocated. They call us the
fearless. They call our love, blind.

~

You cannot love without knowing despair. We all go through moments where we question the life we have. We try and figure out the why and not the what. Then a sudden turn makes life's rollercoaster our favourite ride to be on, as we begin to love each accelerated moment, hoping it would pause for us to soak it in.

~

Love is important to begin something, but respect is always needed to grow.

You will have days when you love them more than you understand the meaning of this mystery. Then you will have days when you just want them to evaporate because you haven't been so mad at anyone ever!

It's important to fall in love. But we need to make sure that love is one of the seats in this rollercoaster you both sit on. There will be bumpy rides.

~

'Have you ever punched a wall?'

'No.'

'Well, that's love. You go in for the punch knowing it will hurt, knowing it will stay with you either as a sensation of uncomfortable comfort or as a scar. Yet once you connect, you go hard because you don't want to have to punch again.

That is love.'

(vii)

Timeless

Despite all the time we spent together, we remained separate identities. We didn't morph into one. I don't think I'd be able to stand her if she became like me! I still question her patience a lot, to be able to bear me! We remained the individuals we fell in love with. That's what kept it fresh.

~

She loved me even when I didn't love myself. At times
I wonder if we fall in love with someone just so they
can love us when we can't love ourselves.

~

We were young, and we were in love.
And as young lovers are, we believed everything
we said we'd do.

~

Her face reminded me of unexpected rain. It was calming to see but the closer you got to it, the more it got to you. Unprepared and intrigued, each step made me more vulnerable to the uncertainties she brought with her. Like a freshly wet floor, there were no blemishes interrupting her beauty. The depth of it was a mystery, one I impatiently waited to unravel. Standing alone, she tried to blend in the silence of the night, not realizing that people with her aura stand out in a room filled with an entire city. A gaze sharp as a laser stared at the emptiness I assumed her thoughts filled and I longed to find myself within those thoughts, just to learn more.

~

She was poetic beauty.
Exactly the kind of person that made it easy to
understand love songs and even sadness.

~

Her eyes had the power to hold my attention for as
long as she demanded.
Her words had the depth to resonate for hours after
they were spoken.
Her touch had the elegance to linger within me
for days.
Her absence had the pain to be felt for a lifetime.

~

That feeling when you realize you're in love.
We always tend to see that moment as the past because
when it happens, boom!
You're not in control of yourself. Not even the slightest.
I'm assuming being shot is the same feeling. In the
moment, you have no control and right after, you know
that control will never be in your hands.

~

You know why falling in love is such a beautiful concept? Because we choose who to fall in love with and someone else chooses to fall in love with us. To be able to find one person we love who loves us back makes this a gamble that is beyond any lottery.

~

For every flower in this world, there is a lover waiting
to give it to his muse.

For every flower in this world, there is a lover waiting
to receive it.

~

Ever want to feel powerful? Fall in love.

Ever want to feel powerless? Fall in love.

Love has a way of making even the most powerful man's legs quiver. Shake like a lonesome leaf on an autumn tree. A whisper away from being free against its will.

Love has a way of making us dream beyond the capacity of a dream and making us experience reality like nothing else can.

(viii)

Landslide

Now darling,
Open your eyes and see we're falling,

Out of these memories,
So why can't you stop us,

Keep our focus,
Isn't that what love is?

So, don't you worry,
I'll wake us up from this,

Nightmares where 'us' turned to you and I,
But promise me that this is the end,
Of this chase and in the bend,

We will start walking again as us,
Because I'm falling into the trap,

And I'm afraid that you will forget about the times we
used to speak in future tense.

~

And . . . Perhaps Love

Here I am waiting,
Waiting for your call,

Here I am staying,
Far above the fall,

If only you saw me,
If only you heard,

You'd see the window,
The window of our world,

Now I am standing,
Above the waterfall,

Drowning and breathing,
Here for the long haul,

Don't you worry,
That's my job to do,

What we have is reserved for two,
What we have is for me and you,

Here I am far above the fall,
If only you saw me, you'd know it all,

You'd see the window,
You'd see the pain,

See the waterfall gushing through my brain,
Don't you worry,

That's my job to do,
What we have is reserved for me and you.

~

Riding on the waves of our stories,
No pain, there's only glory,
But now I see nothing but the end.

~

In this moment I want time to pause and yet in this moment as she rests on my shoulder to sleep, I want time to play every moment we have in store because with each press of her face on my shoulder, I fall in love with the idea of being in love with her.

In the train, the sun burned through the cheap cotton of the curtains used as a makeshift sunscreen, dust particles orbited around us as she slept on the adjoining seat. Before she closed her eyes, there was anger looming with hints of sadness turning her hazelnut eyes maroon with a red that is associated with the pain love brings us.

'This isn't how it should have been,' her voice quivered, shaking with confusion of not knowing how it really should be.

~

The most powerful weapon in the world is love.
Not when you use it but when you take it away.
Steal love from someone and you've turned them into
a monster.

(ix)

Throwing in the Towel

'Why is it that every story about love is so hard to begin
and even harder to cope with at the end?'

The other person thinks as though scanning answers
through a textbook which explains the unexplainable.
The same person continues ranting like a tap bleeding
each drop of pain stored within.

'Why does the pain feel new each time but the
memories older with each thought?'

The listener immediately realizes that at times silence
provides the best answer and at times letting another
person ask several questions gifts them the answer.

'It kills me to think of her and it kills me to try and not to. Funny thing, this love. You can't hate it and you're always scared to love it.'

Like a drip, love feeds its doses in a painful pause.

~

I still take long-drawn breaths when I think of her.
But now they leave me with a bitter taste of sadness.

Today, you appeared in my dream. For the very first
time. Reinstating why it is called a dream, I woke up
to a bed that was half as occupied, longing to go back
to sleep.

~

I didn't know she was the one and to be very honest,
I still don't know, but I'm willing to spend all our lives
solving this puzzle together.

~

I dreamt of you last night. I'm not sure if that is unfair to me or if it is unfair to you but it is definitely unfair. Nobody likes a tease. Seeing you for a split second is a tease that causes a lifelong craving and nothing but turning this to reality can fill this void. You didn't speak. You were just there. Still, almost lifeless yet I could feel your soft skin against my parched fingertips. Aching to hold you, not just brush against you like it were an accident.

Whenever I am in pain, physical that is. I don't rub the hurt. I simply retrace the night we spoke, non-stop, only to reach a conclusion neither of us agreed with. I recall the tears that we refused to shed in each other's presence because we both wanted to be strong for the other. It was ironic because only a few hours later we had to be strong for ourselves. Where's the motivation in that? Just the mere glimpse of that night, imprinted beneath the shutters of my eyes, subsides any physical pain.

You told me the amount you're willing to hurt for someone is the amount you love them and today I no longer feel I exist.

Would I sleep again if the dream were to continue? I'd opt for the soundest sleep, comatose if possible, to get another shared moment with you.

Asleep or not, it was always dreamlike. The agony appears when I realize this dream is a memory which gets as distant with time as the possibility of another one being created.

So I cause myself physical pain, not self-inflicting harm but the clawing of my own nail because of a reflexive impulse taking me to the future we tread on.

~

Why does loss of love make a writer out of a person?

Because while she is with you, all you do is absorb what you hope remains as fond memories and isn't written as content needed to come to terms with the past.

~

I go back to old pictures, as if trying to recap before we meet again.

~

The reality love provides us with is so intimidating, it makes it seem almost unreal. Love really does mean pain, for most of its time but pain comes at a cost. The cost being, love. Which immediately makes this entire situation a catch 22, one everybody aches to obtain.

I knew I was in love. Damn, I knew for sure I was in love. But now, I know there is no extent, no measure, no boundary this love knows. It's like an infant trying to understand its bearings. Continuously growing, with no thought of a limit. I thought I understood love but it doesn't really have a definition, just like it doesn't have any filter.

~

She used to ask me what all I could do for love. I never
knew the answer while she was around. Now that she
isn't around, I seem to have all the answers. Clueless
like a child solving a puzzle, I don't know where
to start.

My only hope is she asks me what all I'd do now.

This time, I will let my actions do the talking.

~

Her eyes looked at me but saw through a layer. Till this day I don't know what that protective sheet was. Mine gazed at her, the same way they do to pictures, which act as the only souvenir our time gifted us. I look at her, and I feel invincible. Herculean as well, and with that power came irresponsibility where I saw a future. She was the protagonist in every scenario of my life. Yet I am a part of this solo act that impatiently waits for her to join in. She wasn't supposed to be a cameo. A cameo so beautiful takes over the entire film, and words won't do justice to the script she helped me envision.

Now I walk with both hands free. I had trained myself to endure the cold in one hand, while the other was used to holding hers. No longer walking slowly, I stride through each step, with a glimmer of hope that there is a beginning somewhere.

~

And . . . Perhaps Love

I took it for granted that it was meant to be. After all,
giving it your all is all it takes.

Putting everything in one basket is a choice you'll
ultimately have to make.

Wandering, not searching for any answers,
I carry a bag filled with questions addressed to you.

Free up your calendar, this could take a while,
A mere mile,
In comparison to what I'd sign up for.

One step away from one leap too far,
Are you good at puzzles?
I'm not.
Some help would be needed to glue this jar.

Forgotten leftovers, what was is scattered to rust,
Anxiety guards the door, letting nothing else in,
Slamming me inside, like a never-ending gust.

Where to now?
Don't say the choice is mine to make.
I had a map in hand,
Navigating through another only seems a mistake.

I'll continue to stand here,
Like a broken clock, maybe the same time will
reappear,
But will you bring the answers along?
Standing in a crowd I thought was my own,
Will you direct me to the lost and found?
That could be holding the answer to the question of
where all that was, will belong.

If I needed one question solved,
Will you be the detective and crack this case?
Will you solve the cube, that's causing these crevices on
my face?

At the beginning or the end,
Whichever part of the journey this can defend,
I catch my breath, not sure what to make,
After all, wasn't giving it your all, all it was going
to take?

~

And . . . Perhaps Love

Didn't you read the story of the man,
Who once knew what love is,
And now he's trying to learn how to stand?

But didn't you get the memo?
Didn't you hear the whispers?
They were screams of laughter not long ago,
Listen closely and you'll hear life telling you where to go.

High as a kite, drowning deep below,
Searching for distractions,
Avoiding our internal interactions,
I swim against tides sweeping me into waves that never
stop to grow.

Did you watch him walk intoxicated?
They say he is trying to find the same sensation
she created,
But now he walks robbed in an infatuation you only
get once,
Yet he is living the rest of his life hoping it'll come,
Safe to say the lover is now a dunce.

Who once knew what love is,
And now he's trying to learn how to stand,
Because the lover is now a dunce.

As he walks alone,
He watches the window glow,
And she's standing there,
With her man and his stare,
Cut through the times,
Of when she was mine,
Of when we were back in time.

Didn't you read the story of the man,
Who once knew what love is,
And now he's trying to learn how to stand,
Because the lover is now a dunce.

~

And . . . Perhaps Love

Skimming through old pictures,
Watching them go live,
Today we're walking in the rain,
Today we're soaking the sunlight.

Flipping through filters,
I saw none when it came to us,
That smile was a smile,
Those words were meant to last.

When did you know,
What I know now?
And when did you know,
I'll be back in the crowd?

It becomes a game of tug of war,
But I entered with no armor,
I find bruises that will last a lifetime,
With resilience for an eternity more to garner.

~

I'm thinking of you and it needs to go.
Of the times we walked aimlessly next to the water,
Comfortable despite being lost.

Of the times we fought in the open,
Knowing we'd always make up in private,
Yet I think of you each time I laugh,
Because instinctively I look right,
And try and find you there,
Hoping one day you would be laughing by my side,
And these moments here would be a long nightmare,
Or a game of hide and seek,
In which I finally win,
In which we finally win.

~

Oh, my sweet drug,
My nectar,
A secret desire,
I shout in my mind,
Hoping you hear what I desire and seek to find.

(x)

For You, from Yours

It was the beginning that brought me to the end. Nothing would have prepared me for what I have been grateful to have felt. Nothing is going to prepare me for what I will feel. The thought of it beginning would have been frightening if I knew what the end would be like. But now that I know the journey, I'd do it countless times over. I don't believe two people are meant to be together. I am a believer they work towards making every force realize they are not meant for anyone else. You called me names, associated me with everything you love, and I started loving everything you did and soon I loved the person you made me. I am not sure if this means I will soon despise the person in the mirror but I'm sure I won't be able to acknowledge the emptiness on all sides. From one step short of going down on one knee to scrambling for pieces on the floor, I wish I was good at puzzles because I can't get myself to pick up the pieces in life I thought were glued for this time and always. I wanted us to last forever and that has led to a life-altering change; the change in the perspective that the term you and I will forever remain sounds incomplete without putting us in a frame.

For you, from yours.

~

'If you've ever truly loved will you know that it hurts
more to love than not to.'

RECAP

(i)

Recap

It was in this moment I knew I was in love,
Watching you stare in the distance,
As I saw an endless distance with you.

It was in that moment that I died a hundred deaths,
When you smiled,
I knew it was time to confess.

It was when you looked away,
I mustered up the courage,
That it was time to say.

It was, and now it isn't,
Life plays its game,
Nobody said it would be pleasant.

It was and it might be,
Hope,
An endless drug, making you believe in eternity.

It was a day ago,
It is a day away,
Her laughter echoes in the silence,
Cutting through each thought,
She always finds her way.

It was in that moment that I knew,
I signed up for a life anew,
Of firsts and lasts but everything shared,
It was, now it isn't,
Yet every part of me continues to care.

~

I was in the middle,
Feet numbing from the pain of going nowhere,
Swollen by the conviction of wanting to go nowhere.

You were at the bend,
I didn't know if that was the beginning or the end,
But you stood in the distance,
Yet you couldn't have been closer if you tried.

We were floating,
Neither here nor there,
Still there was no urgency in our movement,
As long as we were floating together.

~

The other day this woman walked into my life. Then she turned around and kept walking away. As she walked, I stayed exactly where I was standing, motionless because where I was when she was there was exactly how I imagined it to be. My feet didn't move because I was never prepared to lose a moment I didn't think I'll be able to achieve. A mere glimpse is all it seems like now after years of being under the same umbrella we called ours. Now each second drags itself slowly, parched for what walked away while I stand scared questioning if I'd ever have the courage to quench this thirst again.

(ii)

Unscramble

I've had a drink,
Maybe more than one,
But I'm not drunk,
I'm finally one,
One with my thoughts,
Not scared to acknowledge the truth,
That masks the lies,
That covers what I should think too,
Nothing replaces you.

~

Don't know where to start,
So, I'm sitting where we started,
The same place where I thought we'd begin,
Instead this spot is from where you departed.

I lost at love, but the love isn't lost,
Empty-handed with a filled heart,
What was a gain is now a cost.

The water continues to flow as it did when we sat
together,
Each drop screaming in my ears,
The ripples aren't alone as they quiver.

Wherever you are, isn't this spot we claimed for two,
Didn't think there would be a world,
Where we'd go back to separating
What's mine and what's just for you.

Eyes closed or eyes open,
There isn't darkness but a haze,
Confused and deluded,
The mind stumbles trying to find its way.

What happened to the future we spoke of?
What happened to the past we created?

And . . . Perhaps Love

It all happened too fast, why does it sink so slow?
What was once one is now segregated.

There isn't much sense in this moment,
I wonder if it's a prank played for every moment I tried
too hard,
Now I'm left with stamina for the eternity we promised,
But life has played its trump card.

~

You're my peaceful chaos
I walk into this darkness to see,
Everything that was and won't be.

You're my calm storm,
I run through,
Hoping the loop will mingle me and you.

You're my silent cheer,
I hold on,
Wondering what time will adorn.

You're my painful remedy,
I apply with no apprehension,
A glimmer of delusion pointing towards an extension.

You're my right and wrong,
I watch the clock take away every moment we could share,
Reminding me you're you and I'm me,
What's yours is yours, not mine to be,
You're the silence, despite my cheer,
You're the calm, I'm the storm I fear,
You're the light and peace, but not for me to release,
You're you, and that is all it took,
For a wish, that this would turn into you and me.

~

And . . . Perhaps Love

A continuous mirage,
Creating trails from breadcrumbs,
That are now stale.

This is a conversation with the universe,
Each and every one of us,
Currently on bail.

Walking towards a pathway,
That narrows into a funnel,
Filtering us through an unchartered channel,
As we dig through this tunnel.

I walk through the gates,
That introduced me to you,
Standing with a smile,
Knowing I have no clue,
Of what lies ahead,
And what truth will unfold,
But I'd walk through these gates again,
Because it was the smile that got me sold.

The artist that paints these mirages,
Is a delude known as our past,
Holding the brush in fear,

Sanil Sachar

A fool to believe,
Grasping tight will make yesterday last.

Yet you find yourself thinking of back then,
This time painting a new image,
Labelled 'what if',
Making you wonder if you're better off as a mirage.

~

I tell them why you're gone,
Trying to make sense of what is wrong,
Solving the puzzle of why I'm here,
Explaining an algorithm that alone we're okay.

(iii)

Perpetual Perplexity

I wonder where our days have gone,
I wonder when time will make us strong,
I wonder what you'll be doing there,
I wonder who will catch our air,
I wonder, I wonder, I wonder,
But never why,
Because you're my darling,
A dream of yesterday,
Tomorrow, a lie,
So, I wonder, I wonder,
I wonder when,
When our time will come,
I vote for no end,
I wonder, I wonder, I wonder how,

And . . . Perhaps Love

How we will live this life,
If we can't pause the now,
And 'forever'.

~

A recurring tape continues to play on,
Conversations turn to voices,
As I know exactly where each whisper is from.

Images flash,
No longer will the story continue,
Left being an observer,
With an album,
Only I go through.

All the questions pile up,
An exam with no grades,
Beginning to figure a reason,
Before the meaning fades.

A haze covers the distance,
A blessing in disguise,
Leaves pile on the ground,
I wonder if it's here what is lost will be found.

~

And . . . Perhaps Love

Talk to me, you beautiful lie,
Tell me everything that'll work a smile,
Whisper with no boundary,
Embrace me with no restriction,
I am your puppet,
Waiting to be strung by deception.

Sing to me of times that'll never come,
Waltz with me and let hope lead us to the undone,
Lying here with me as we lie awake,
The midnight oil burns memories that never saw the
light of day.

Bring me to the future,
One where I promised and you nodded in belief,
Carry me through those lanes plastered with images we
will never see,
Gift me that perfect lie,
I'm not scared to drown in it,
My biggest fear wasn't that I'll die.

Lift me above the crooked truth,
That learns as it limps its way to days it never knew,
Caress me with the soothing lie,
That which will never stay,
A discomfort I'll never deny.

Stare at me with those eyes,
Stare at me and spell out each lie,
Of times that never saw their time,
Or moments that never got to live,
Amongst each other where they would be impatient
to meet,
Tell me those beautiful lies,
I am numb,
Perfectly ripe to be deceived.

Talk to me, you beautiful lie,
I'm all yours,
It's been a while.

(iv)

In the Distance

I saw you from the corner of my eye,
And wondered if you saw me,
But as I turned to face you,
You had gone,
No longer in sight,
Now left to the imagination of my mind.

I spoke of you in the future tense,
And the fondness of memories we will make,
Foolish to believe the present will lead me there,
Scrambling on the ground, finding pieces of the past to
hold on to,
Time has its own ways to make you feel powerless.

I thought of you, standing at the crossroads of who
I was and who I don't know I'll become,
Wondering what I'll leave behind in this transition
for one,
Fully aware you'll accompany me,
While I lose sight of who I was, as you find your place
within who I become.

~

And . . . Perhaps Love

Words from the past, sit on my lap,
Dried-up pages,
Crisp as the memories they spur,
Become heavier as dry eyes begin to blur.

What was written then is still true,
Was I lying, speaking of someone I thought I knew?

Hands tremble,
Flipping the brittle pages of the past,
Each sentence holds on,
Silent cries make passing moments last.

Eyes constantly gazing,
Concentration that has no control over the mind,
No point living in the past,
Then why is all of me walking behind?

(v)

Last Call for Departure

Sadness from loss only comes from the happy memories linked to who is now a companion of the past. We huddle around the dining table, wiping our tears as they gush uncontrollably. Everyone narrates their favourite story only to realize each reminiscence is a personal favourite. While one narrates, the others listen earnestly waiting for their moment to show off a side to the being only they thought they knew. Greedy to let out their shared moments in a fear that keeping it within any longer will turn fact into fiction. Over the years, each story is bound to get altered by made-up additions. Simply because with time, we feel the longer the story, the more protected we are from forgetting it. In truth, no story is ever as powerful as the reverberations it causes within the narrator because the power of words will never outplay the impact of love that can't be spoken of.

~

She knew it was time for her to leave, yet she waited for me to plead, harder than I ever did, as I hoped I would be heard by gods I haven't ever spoken to.

~

I took it for granted that it was meant to be. After all,
giving it your all is all it takes.

I taped all the torn bits. Every scratch and each rip.

Defaced, what I loved changed but how I loved didn't.

(vi)

Bitter Aftertaste

At times, we're so caught up in the plans we make that we forget about the reasons we made them. It was a similar case for us. We planned our lives like architects working on every intricacy. Completely disregarding any possibility of an unforeseen circumstance acting as a tornado over our plans. Lovers are dreamers for this very reason. Conveniently forgetting that any external reality can take over internal thoughts.

~

She used to give me all the answers and now I have a question and there is nobody who can answer it.

~

Draw me the picture framed as a hope,
Hold my hand as it shivers,
Adding to each stroke.

You never said this is how it would be,
I never thought it would be this way;
Times know how to challenge the defined,
Once holding a map,
Now, I'm astray.

The wind blows cold on my face,
But I've been immune to the very pain,
Sins from the past,
Now cocktails through droplets in each vein.

~

I loved her, I never questioned how much until I was made to realize it the day she wasn't there anymore. There was no point in evaluating then. The calculations made no sense when love had no place to rest.

~

Me.

You seek.
I can't hide.
You preach.
I can't guide.
You treat.
I can't imbibe.
You see.
I can't drive.
You breathe.
I can't survive.
You feel.
I am alive.

~

I don't think the problem is that you're not here,

I don't see the solution anywhere,

I find myself thinking about what is clear,

That one day I'll see you there,

And you'll be standing at the bar,

With him, holding his cigar,

Wearing a smile that used to be,

Exclusive to you and me.

~

It becomes impossible to flip the calendar each month. Every turn of the page reminds me of a month that has passed. Another month, where the only new element is the difference in its name.

~

If love is the reason for disaster, why do we cry
for love?

(vii)

When it Rains, it Pours

I want to fall in love, but I have no courage to fall out,
and I possess no willpower to fall in. I am stuck in
the middle. Playing observer and actor to these waves
that occasionally drown me in an ocean of adrenaline.
An adrenaline rush I don't know how to deal with in
isolation from the pain love gifts you.

~

This is the story of a broken heart. It's crushed. Let me rephrase that . . . it's crushing. Slowly, like sand slipping out of a tight grip, it's losing its place and scattering too far apart. I loved her and she knew that. This was supposed to be the easy bit. Instead, she used my love as ammunition, holding it against my head. Holding me ransom to my own feelings, which are stunned beyond belief, losing faith in the word love, let alone what it stands for.

Will I love again? I hope so. Love is always different; it can never be the same which is why it's always so exciting and always so scary. Yet what we had can never be replicated. It was short and no longer is it sweet. A poisonous aftertaste because of the advantage she took of the love I gave her. So much of it, people would call me a fool and I was one. Every lover is a bit off their head but to love without any control, never knowing if it will come back, that is the sign of a fool. I loved her. She knew. Oddly, this became my foe and not our ally.

~

When we lose something old, something new comes and replaces it. But we don't want the new and the new doesn't want us.

In this moment, we are vulnerable, exposed and a second away from destruction. Open like an uncovered gash that is aching to become a scar, but you never let it heal. You keep picking at it, in the hope you can make it go back to 'normal'.

However, after all that peeling and attempts to redeem it, what started as a cut is now unrecognizable. Turning you into something new but all you want is the old.

~

'Do you write?'
No, I'm a writer in my heart though. I like what I see
but I am scared I might end up writing what others
can't see.

~

I want to write us a book. You said you wanted to read it and here I am short of words. Writing, with the hope that these alphabets will pacify the confusion that brews within. I don't believe in time because it's deceptive. Unlike some of us, it can't make its mind up. When we're away it ticks painfully slowly and when we're sitting together, it moves so quick, you wonder if it is making up for the times it felt as though it had paused. One of us doesn't like rollercoasters but aren't we all a part of one? Each shining light in front turns out to be useless. On the contrary, each dark alley gets us to an adrenaline rush we crave for over and over again. Hope keeps us going. It keeps us believing that time will pass for the experiences that makes this time fly. We've run several marathons together, half of them on a treadmill, the other on paths some call a slope. How hard is another marathon to run if you've already trained? I want to write a book, a story or even a word that describes this. This for now is a sensation that hopes with confidence. Confidence stirred by two core ingredients, time and experience.

~

We're all trying to break through.
You and I are similar that way.
We keep asking for more.
We're a greedy race, us humans.
We'd demand more even if we get the stars.

~

In a different world,
The distance would be a mystery,
In a different world,
This would be easy.

~

At first, I'd look into your eyes skipping countless blinks. Now I have to make sure I don't look into them for too long because I no longer have the privileges we had back then.

~

A slow motion never seemed to move this fast,
The tracks are fresh,
I've been on this path,
One where the clouds turn to shapes indicating a sign,
I thought back then I knew nothing,
Yet today I feel blind.

This carriage has written countless stories,
None of them promised to be endless,
Yet they run through these tracks like a child in a
playground,
A lover then,
A delude now,
Experience gained through a judgement that is the
farthest from being sound.

We've been here countless silences ago,
Pondering on words that didn't ever flow,
You've made promises and I rallied back with a few
more to list,
That yearns to live its time,
Neither of us have the courage to inform it no
longer exists.

Speed catches up but it has its way,
Creeping up from angles,

And . . . Perhaps Love

Lurking through a delusion I learn never to obey,
Swimming past tides we cruised through with ease,
The simpler times went unnoticed,
Oblivious I thought they would never decrease.

The wind pushes the train,
The train pushes the track,
The track pushes through seconds,
The seconds push me like a pendulum to and from
the past.

These windows reflect a smile,
A smile that doesn't match the eyes,
Those that see the moment,
Those that recognize the lies,
While the slow-motion races fast,
I hold onto those paths,
That always come back to comfort in silence,
But never live to last.

~

We're playing hide and seek,
But we're both seeking,
We're playing hard to get,
In search of a meaning.

DEMOLITION

(i)

Demolition

Wasted.
Doing anything to be busy.
Wasted.
Standing in the distance to stay safe.
Wasted.
Being wiped away by my own expectations.
Wasted.
Hoping to love nothing and feel no frustrations.
Deluded.

~

There's a nothingness in my chest,
Resting like a stone wrapped around a body,
Heading down the ocean, to contest,
For the longest time without a breath,
That was once pure.

~

At first, I wrote because it helped me speak my mind. Now, I find it hard to write because it's my mind speaking.

(ii)

Comfort in the Lies

Standing on water,
Swimming in the sky,
They say it's impossible,
Stubbornness in the veins, insisting we give it a try.

Dancing with the devil,
Waltzing in front of the mirror,
What's the difference?
The devil's thoughts are clearer.

Hazy days and clear nights,
Peaceful wars, internal fights,
The rhythm doesn't match the hands on the keyboard,
I look up to a grey sky,
Is that the dark lord?

And . . . Perhaps Love

Mist continues to form,
Or maybe those are polluted eyes,
Reflections start to form,
A delusion filled with mirages,
There's comfort in resting in these lies.

A stinging pain never hurts,
As much as the anticipation,
The itch always worked,
Ramping up the chaos.

Magicians never amazed me,
They merely paint the truth for a flash,
A psychic should turn up,
To study the complexities foreseeing the crash.

No one walks on water,
Nobody swims in the sky,
The decisions are as stable as an earthquake,
The calm always welcomes the storm,
Despite how much you try.

~

I was frustrated. An emotion that seemed more normal than what defines 'normal'. Waiting for another sentiment to wash over, I sat with a thumping chest, bursting out to overcome the anxiety associated with survival. We never know what's coming our way. Yet we are surprised by this phenomenon. It's almost like we believe ourselves to be magicians, able to predict the future. Our actions lead us to the next day, but they will never draw it out completely. Even the top artists in the world can't perfectly sketch over a trace. We're merely beginners at this craft, first-timers to life. No Picasso to our own existence, we just about manage to hold the pen to our lives without our hands quivering for too long through each stretch.

(iii)

Aimless Pursuit

He waits staring at the seconds tick
But they only move fast on the clock.

~

Traversing through uncharted territories that haven't
seen the light of day,

Wandering through a forest glimmering, always one
step away,

Skipping over countless footsteps that might have
the answer,

Of how to choose: either to play choreographer
or dancer.

Shadows lurk in the distance, gauging every fault,

Knowing fully well, we have no options to default,

A game with only one lifeline,

An arcade cramped with stumbling minds,

Clueless to the fact that everyone else is clueless.

An arm's length away,

With every stretch, the mark leads us astray,

And . . . Perhaps Love

Of where to go and where you've come from,

Seldom forgetting, the point you rest on.

Mist masks what where when how and why,

A curtain, teasing to reveal itself,

Little do we know this moment will stretch, as you
reach for the sky,

But clouds form shapes laughing at your intent,

Legs weigh heavier, still you climb your mythical
mountain,

Until you know, it has no end.

Welcome to the mythical mountain.

~

If I had the chance to make a confession and find my way through heaven, I'd rather stay quiet and take the stairway to hell.

~

And . . . Perhaps Love

Lining up in our slaughterhouse,
One stands tall, the other knows it will fall,
Weighing their relevance in the times to come,
One is worth the wait,
One can't wait till it has begun.

Judgement day,
A daily ordeal,
Decisions line up to be sacrificed,
Until one can be revealed,

Stop.
We hope, we pray, we burn candles in the day,
Desperation doesn't stand strong,
Each day contemplating its relevance,
Yet we live,
Perching in the shadows painted by complexities,
Concocted to land on an epiphany,
When all you want is a life where each decision gets a
chance,
An attempt to prove it's the lesser of the evils,
Nobody said there is just one devil,
Let me make each option compete,
Nobody warned me, there is only one level.

~

A million names, a million faces,
Countless roads, endless traces,
Her smile, an ocean-deep memory instilled within,
Hiding in the depths of nostalgia,
Screams inside wave to the world as a grin.

Being crazy isn't fun, I take back this childhood cry,
Avoiding mirrors isn't the way the battle is won,
Counting each breath as a fresh start makes you
question:
To live or to die?
Living doesn't sound so easy and death doesn't sound
too hard,
Ideas crash to the floor, leaving options as to which one
to disregard.

Labelled by names, constantly playing games,
The mind is a rollercoaster, open 24/7,
Mouth sealed unable to share, like a pact kept till
the heavens.

~

Each night before bed I look at a red light as it
stares back at me from the switch of the television.
Exchanging glances, it screams like a sign with just one
message: that I am in desperate need of a sign.

~

Waves crash against the rocks,
For the waves, the rocks are a hindrance,
For the rocks, the waves a constant nuisance.
Now the waters dry out,
And the rocks sit still,
Wondering what their worth is.

~

Let me see,
In the silence of my chaos,
Let me breathe,
As the winds change direction,
Let me free,
While I sit still knowing I can go,
This is me,
Or me that I recognize today.

~

The sound of the creeping fan hums even louder to an idle mind. No mind should be idle, not for a moment. That's the closest we come to being defined as the living dead.

(iv)

Tumbleweed

'It's all in the head.'
But how is that a solution?
It'll fade away,
'It's just confusion.'

What makes you so certain?
Are you holding the remote?
If so, pass it over,
So, I can finally decide,
What is right and what is left?
What can't stay within,
And that I have no choice but to digest.

'It's a phase.'
Since when did you become the architect of this maze?

'What are you thinking?'
I'll answer if you promise to prevent this sinking,
And don't ask me what,
Definitely not the why,
I see options around me,
They all say I give it a try,
One more time and they promise the dream,
Nothing too fancy,
Just a good night's rest,
With no thoughts coming in between.

'That's all you want?'
For now, that's a leap too far,
So yes, let's take what we get,
Closed doors inside scream to open themselves ajar.

~

I have with me a sword,
It has two sides,
One is sharp,
The other is sharper.
It holds pent-up energy,
Rubbing against each other with venomous speed,
Preparing for devastation.

~

I thought about you today. I shouldn't have. Not because you aren't mine and I'm not yours but because these thoughts delude me into believing we are one another's for the entirety of those seconds while I fixate about you.

~

'You knew you were making a mistake, why did you go
ahead with it?'
At times, we fight knowing we will lose, just so we can
be near a winner.

~

I've never felt love like the love she has left me with.
Consequently, I haven't felt such remorse from a void
no one can fill.

(v)

Wide Asleep

I'm wide awake,
I'm wide asleep,
Staring at the stars,
Hoping they start to speak,
Make a word, a single peep,
This one-way conversation is going nowhere,
Like a merry-go-round,
Comes straight back to my head,
A chemical lab concocting newer thoughts,
Turning humans into bots.

~

A hallucination,
Despite the distance, the waves match,
Meeting at the same station.

A fixation,
Only at the start, leaving a scar,
Without hesitation.

Completely abstract,
Leading to a thrill.

~

When things start moving against you, you don't realize it. That's the defensive mechanism in a person trying to protect them when it is doing the exact opposite. But soon, little sparks turn to big fires.

(vi)

Implosion

I'm procrastinating. It seems to be the new-age replacement of 'I have a lot to do and I want to do it all but at the same time I don't want to do it, because it takes effort, so I'll do it later and pretend like it was harder than it is'. So, I'm sitting here, holding my pen in one hand, with earphones in my ear, shuffling the pen through my fingers, pretending to be creatively thinking while, in fact, my fingers are moving like a dancer to the song playing on repeat. Yes, on repeat because I am afraid of any change while I procrastinate. The comfort in this still motion keeps me from doing what I want to do, as I sit watching a blank piece of paper wondering why I am not doing what I want to do. It all sounds like a riddle in my head but I am too occupied to solve it because I am procrastinating. My

mind is shuffling, like an iPod with old songs, it thinks
of her, and the time before that and a moment that
didn't take place and a conversation I should have had.
It skims through instances that set rage within, making
these thoughts heavier than they are, causing them
to be ever so difficult to slip away. What made her
appear in this maze? Is she a metaphor for loss? Is loss a
symbol of a repeated motion? Is motion a nag towards
the stillness I am in? I continue to be questioned by
my own questions and yet there are no answers. Not
because the answers don't exist. Simply because no one
in this room for one makes the effort to give an answer
because I am procrastinating.

~

Don't let intoxicated thoughts take over your
sober ambitions.

~

I have become the kind of man who wakes up thinking
I got up on the wrong side. Blaming the day when
the shower is cold. I blamed everything, when all I
needed to do was take charge and be on the driver's seat
for once.

~

Have you ever said something and wondered what
you said?
Not because you don't believe it or it's a lie.
Just simply because what you said is so true,
it scares you.

~

And . . . Perhaps Love

Lately, reality has been making me second guess,
Lately, I've been confused,
Lately, an invisible load rests on my chest.

Strangely, I question myself more,
Strangely, I think I've lost the key,
Strangely, I don't panic being locked outside the door.

Now, I see more with my eyes open,
Contemplate even more as I blink,
Walk fully aware, I'm bound to sink.

There is a remedy locked somewhere,
In a chest of the past,
A gaze away from a constant stare.

Hazy like a cloud,
This mind begins to float away,
There was colour on this palate; why then is the
brightest shade now grey?

Steep yet safe,
A mountain to climb in this journey,
There is a mist of uncertainty in each new step,
I'm not here to watch,
I've just begun.

~

A man with nothing to go back to is never scared to die.
Not being afraid of death is the best form of attack.

EXPLORATION

(i)

Exploration

I met you at the bend,
Between where I was and where I wanted to be,
And suddenly, I didn't want to be there alone,
So, I walked slower, hoping you'd catch up,
And that one day we'd be at a bend, between where we
are and where we want to be.

~

We're all searching,
Like wanderers lost at sea,
In a blizzard filled with our expectations,
We're all searching.

We're all choking,
Like a novice dipped under water,
In a haze consumed by our greed,
We're all choking.

We're all overthinking,
Not realizing,
Even the day doesn't know what's in store.

We're all silently screaming,
Our pleas masked by a rehearsed smile,
Voices confined to the echoes in our mind, we're
screaming,
But they're nothing more than whispers in this jungle.

We're all dreaming,
Like a treadmill,
Going nowhere,
We skip the present,
Jumping from past to future,

And . . . Perhaps Love

We're dreaming,
Looking for a non-existent reason in this
continuous loop.

~

When you have nowhere to go, you're never in a rush,
But time finds the weaker stick,
And pushes it through each street,
That calls your name gently,
While you carelessly skip with your feet.

When you have nowhere to be,
Every destination is a transit,
Every minute is a plane,
Preventing you from coming to a standstill.

When you have no one to see,
Nothing fills your hunger,
They're all mirages of a better tomorrow,
Today you wear blinders to enjoy the thunder.

When you have nothing to say,
Silence is your biggest foe,
Whispering thoughts, you didn't know.

In times of trouble, you seek another to add to the pile,
We are our own villains,
Wishing the hero in us was more agile,
To extinguish the fire,
As one hand lights the flame,

And . . . Perhaps Love

When you have nothing to do,
Creating a mess to clean seems sane.

In pursuit of finding yourself,
You stop for directions,
Signs that haven't been constructed,
Seeking advice, ensuring an end to spontaneity,
Yet you tread with nowhere to go, no one to see,
Nothing to do, unaware of who and how to be,
In a relentless search for a destination that has no end.

(ii)

Reconstruction

Expectations, an ocean asking for more with
each ripple,
Floating in a mind of a first-time sailor,
Sunsets, sunrise, orange to blue,
Traversing through old and new,
Expectations pile up as waves introducing themselves
with each passing one,
Embracing the tides that can't be undone.

~

You felt it was not going to be your day and gave up?
Funny how people like you think each day is a new set
of cards dealt.
It's not.
We are all dealt one set of cards.
It's how you play the hand over your life that
determines each day.

~

You're shedding your skin,
Vulnerable, being naked,
Rearing to begin,
Stand loose,
Forget the urge to resist,
Call this a new beginning,
Label this your reason to exist.

Let the moment swallow you,
Be one with this fear,
You're as alive as the past you let go off,
While tomorrow will flirt to bring you near.

~

And . . . Perhaps Love

Booze in their blood,
Lust on their minds,
Wanderers, they go by,
A bag filled with wings as they fly.

Faded memories, permanent scars,
We've seen the world,
We've rendered dry every bar.

Take me by the hand,
And I'll show you every street,
Maps don't know their names,
But they'll never forget our feet.

A crimson face, faded memories,
Scars and stamps are our remaining accessory,
Infused with smoke, resembling a hot-air balloon,
Let the wind dictate the direction,
We don't fear losing ourselves,
It's in the darkness we are immune.

Would you walk with me if I told you I was lost?
Would you choose me over an opportunity cost?
Will you wander in circles?
Believing we are finding our way,
Will you stray in the darkness?

In tranquillity, knowing on the other side, we might
be astray,
And this path we tread on will begin anew,
We are all wanderers, the first step is followed by the
second, however, by a countless few.

~

And . . . Perhaps Love

I'm a wall,
This, the comfortable circle.

A pattern that doesn't change,
A sequence, part of the game.

Only one key that'll get me out of this lane,
Which isn't near and neither is it far,

It's here when I close my eyes,
It's here when they're open yet nobody else can see,

That this pattern is now only for me to solve.
A Rubik's cube that doesn't stay in place,

A game of mirrors with a different reflection,
The world revolves, changing its direction,

Round and round in a circle,
The comfortable space, where everything changes,

Yet it all ends the same,
Perched on a pattern that begins to fade,

Resting on the edge, wondering when to be brave,
This is the comfortable circle.

(iii)

Primary Trail

At times I just sit, watching time pass as I stay in the same place. Like being in the middle of the ocean, every wave of time misses me, keeping me far from the shore. In the middle, stuck, not drowning and definitely not floating.

It makes me wonder why life isn't a short story where it all happens quickly. Why are there so many chapters, when only a few words define our entire life?

~

My time is limited,
If you tell me how much I have of it,
I will capitalize on it,
If you tell me how little I have of it,
I will destroy it.

My life is monitored,
If you tell me I am being watched,
I will put on a show,
If you tell I am invisible,
I'll be gone before I hear go.

~

A cry of laughter at one end of the world is always matched by a cry of sadness at the other. Happiness and sadness enter at the same time but from separate doors. While one appears in the present, the other is inspired by the past. Like a coin tossed in the air, the odds of it landing at the same time is nearly impossible, yet we watch it land, hoping we find ourselves at the end of a smile.

~

Life is not about the opportunities you didn't take. It's about those you took because of which, the ones you didn't weren't missed. Life is to be rejoiced at.

~

Sanil Sachar

The biggest lie we tell ourselves in public is that we are adults when in truth we are children in disguise.

~

At times we are old enough to demand something but young enough to get bored by it. This is why it's best to use this transitioning period as a window shopper and not invest in our lives.

~

Judge a man through his anger not during light. Pursue what you seek for in darkness, not during respite.

(iv)

Sunrise Boulevard

As the days end and the calendars open,
Life adds another wrinkle to its mask,
Ageing with each glimpse of how we weigh our future
against the past.

While the clocks repeat the same hand,
In a motion whose speed we decide,
The calendars watch from afar,
Wondering where we want to reside.

The wind blows with echoes and cheers,
Confetti rests on tired feet,
Spirits as high as the spirits take us,
The calendars lean closer to hear what we
have to discuss.

People speak in the future tense,
Goals and endeavours the anthem for all,
It all seems achievable as we discuss in unison,
The calendar showers hope as a free for all.

Rays of the sun seem brighter,
The clouds a pillow to the skies we want to reach,
Where we are is a transit,
The calendar today a propeller getting us to what
we preach.

As the days end, the calendars show a new face,
The seconds and minutes wait for the hours to narrate,
The what, why, when and how,
No need to look any further,
The calendars point to the opportunity that will always
be in the now.

~

And . . . Perhaps Love

Pupils magnified by the moment,
We were never meant to cross paths,
Yet we stare at each other,
With stories of the future and the past,
Because the present belongs to no one.

I see you analysing me,
Searching for scars,
Don't look any further,
We've been brave,
Strong enough to stand here facing each other.

You walk away with no trace,
But I know where you've been,
I am here due to each mistake you deny,
You are here, wondering how many times I repeated
each mistake.

Were we good to ourselves?
Is anyone?
Were we hard on ourselves?
Isn't everyone?
Will we meet again?
Can anyone know for sure?
Will we live through it all?
All this is there to make this living a bit more fun,

And experience tells me,
By the time we know, it'll be too late to say,
So live while you live through it all,
That's what makes us meet,
That's what will make you stand in my place,
Resting on the bridge named the present;
Talking of then and when,
When me meets me.

~

He flew into a world he didn't know,
Colours that haven't been discovered,
Definitions of breathing that haven't been attempted,
Walking into the darkness he saw a prism,
Shades of a rainbow calling his name,
Floating like a balloon with no destination.

Staring into eyes dilated,
Elated,
In bliss.

RECOVERY

(i)

Recovery

Your weakness will manifest wherever you have the most strength to pull yourself back up.

It's times when you're down that you need to see what you've done to get there.

Not what got you down but what you kept up.

Everything you do will have an opportunity cost.

Don't be too careful deciding what to do and what not to do but when you choose to let go of something, make sense of it by making the most of what you kept in return.

Your weakness is only because you're making sense of
what you have and that is where your strength
will unfold.

Falling is a part of this process.

Don't force yourself to stay strong; recoup and
you'll get stronger.

~

Yesterday I was one day away from a new life. Today, each conversation could be the last. It's funny how we plan for every scenario apart from the one being painted by a third-party artist, who has access to your canvas.

It's easy being sad about life and believing nothing good will come from it. In this moment, we need to think of the moment we are in. If it weren't for it, we wouldn't be able to determine the good and the bad.

If you try hard enough, you can make the best moments the worst by demanding it again. Which is why the best moments come once.

When you're the one who can destroy you, that's a cry for help because no one can save you. Don't die for yourself and don't live for yourself. Find a purpose and make the purpose immortal.

(ii)

Befriending the Mirror

If all that you do is for a purpose,
Don't search for a result in the end,
It might disappoint you regardless of the outcome,
The final stretch might offer you a bend.

If every time you fall for one,
Don't stop planning ahead,
It might surprise you,
The future is only content if your present is fed.

If the light shines bright,
Don't shy away,
It's bound to change its focus,
Stay focused, don't let it lead you astray.

And . . . Perhaps Love

If you're rushing but want to stop,
Catch your breath, absorb it all,
No one has conquered anything,
Till you can make peace with your internal brawl.

If time stops as you stare into those eyes,
Stop with it and lose yourself,
To make sense of what the mirror has to say,
Silence once heard fully is bound to take you miles.

If you find clutter taking over the life you lead,
Step back,
It won't slow you,
Remember there's always possibility of everything
better.

~

Look at us go,
Like birds without wings we call every place home,
Look at us dream,
Like believers we wear blinders and jump in to sink,
But now you know,
We're warriors living in a hole,
So, watch us leave,
There will be plenty of us,
But no one like me,
No one like you,
Nothing like this,
Sitting on a ride, I call bliss,
So, watch us go,
Maybe then they'll know,
We're birds growing our wings,
We're that man in the bar waiting to sing,
We're that woman watching the world she owns,
We're everyone that is here to grow,
Look at us go.

(iii)

Waltzing with Equilibrium

It's in this fire that I search for a desire,
What went so fast is taking so long to dissolve,
Time plays its own game,
I'm bound to burn my hand in the hope of going
higher.

~

Lingering, like a man standing on the edge,
Rushing in like a dog playing fetch,
I wait in anticipation of your next step,
Pause time before there's need of help.

Losing the courage to fall out,
Seeking the willpower to fall in,
A seesaw of emotions moves back and forth,
Questions bounce, as though a pendulum within
my skin.

~

I am the culprit of my own sins,
The wrath wraps me into a shell I live within,
Engaging with fear as the tides watch me drown,
The benefactor of my mistakes, each fall I adorn like
a crown.

You'll never see me crumble,
In the ways my mind decides to,
You'll never see me humble,
Wearing a mask of arrogance is my protection.

~

Lying here, fast asleep yet wide awake,
Nothing to lose, yet everything at stake.

In the midst of all this silence, there is a sound,
Despite no movement,
There is a place I'm bound.

Just like a watch,
My time ticks away,
I have two choices,
Utilize each second of this night,
Or lie here unchanged, till the next day.

In the midst of all this silence,
This sound seems clearer than before,
Not only is there movement but that too towards the
open door.

Progress seems slow, but progress nonetheless,
The target seems clearer,
Slowly getting rid of all the mess.

Nothing worth achieving can be achieved without
struggle and a fight,
Only after reaching your destination can you
have respite.

So, I'll drink my head in till I reach the other end,
And I'll get sharper and closer to my goal with each
passing bend.

(iv)

Confusion over Conclusion

People want to be different, yet they are scared to try the new.

This leaves everything old in a safe zone and everything that is to come on the tipping point.

One refusal away from being shunned before it ever sees the light.

~

And . . . Perhaps Love

I see a reflection, run!
Sense a deflection, done.

The gas pipes stop leaking, numb.
Close my eyes but I'm not sleeping, succumb.

Shadows are brighter than the light around my face,
Darkness isn't all that bad,
When what's in offer isn't what you want to embrace.

A halo is a noose, a noose a dead end,
Maybe that's why they refer to it as a short-term friend.

Questions and answers skip around our board,
A chess game with no master,
Experimenting is the rhythm to what will be secured.

Those who know, know better than not to speak,
Those who don't, never stop, gathering believers to
the peak.

A view in sight, never a view we are on,
Progress is an investment we are sold,
Never a landmark, ever since we are born.

I see a reflection, it's me,
I sense a deflection, I can see,
The pipes in my hand, the nozzle on the stand,
The noose an arm's length away,
The chess game still incomplete,
I thank my curiosity, others called OCD,
To stay on and skip,
I rather progress have the better off me.

~

And . . . Perhaps Love

An anchor sets itself on this chest,
Turning into the orchestrator of each breath,
Pull hard, inhale the fumes,
Life's pollution was never meant to be your suit.

A rushing wave,
Leaps over my head,
Luckily, it can't stand high,
Ever since half of me began to melt.

A burning sensation lights the path,
Scattered laces,
In this race for one,
I find myself coming last.

A bridge sprawled ahead of me,
The past and future stand watching as the present
chooses left or right,
The constructor laughing at my misery,
There is no answer inside.

Rain pours down on the trail,
Erasing every hint of where to go,
Grown used to the feeling of being still,
Like a corpse watching his life try again,
Rebooting to a second chance,

Craving another dance,
With life leading the way to death,
Not the other way around,
That number doesn't have a ring to it,
Removing the anchor instead,
Dislodging it from the ground,
Learn to live, even when you are not around.

~

God shows himself in the smallest manners. You see that lonely leaf by the pond. It hasn't drowned yet. It's beating all odds not getting pushed by the wind. That is a sign from God. A sign that even the most helpless beings can be invincible.

~

The smallest open wound can be the most painful
injury because it's real.
That is what the truth is if you pretend it is not true.

~

Lately I've been dodging what I love the most. It's not because my love for it has faded, in fact if anything the value it holds in my life has grown through this distance I have created between us. I've spent time that was dedicated towards it lurking around observing other creations. They are all beautiful in their own right. Stunning work doesn't just emerge from nowhere. It is moulded over time, and through several corrections. Our love for the creation comes predominantly from the tedious process and the hardships of letting go of much that you love but isn't worth your story, in place of holding on to all that you learn to love because it makes more sense for it to stay. Staring at nothingness is a part of the process. Being lonely, despite a cluttered mind and an even more crowded surrounding, makes you question whether what you love is worth the hassle. But then you realize your patience with anything else is almost non-existent when it comes to the effort you are willing to put in finding your comfort spot again. I've been dodging what I love not because the love has faded but because I feel I won't be as good at it or live up to the heights of how good I know it deserves. Still I stare right at it, a blank canvas that could be painted by the most minute details that make it so special to me, and I wonder, if I should write again.

~

There's a freshness in the air,
A stillness urging us to dare,
Pushing limits that didn't know they exist,
The winning strategy remains, we persist.

~

It's been a while since we last spoke,
I haven't asked you how you've been,
Never questioned any road you took,
So, how have you been, my friend?
Feels weird labelling you as one,
When truly I feel we are one,
Yet I demand more from you,
And you hint the same from me,
How have you been?
More importantly how has it been?
A rollercoaster?
A tornado?
A flood of questions unanswered?
A ride that feels too short?
How have you been?
More importantly,
How will you be, as we embark on this journey,
We move so fast we can't see one another,
When we move slow, we don't meet eye to eye,
Last time we spoke, I wouldn't believe any of that you
said you'd do,
But here you are, having done more than you said,
So, don't ask too little of yourself,
Push yourself because staying here is a short present,
Push yourself and ride the waves,

You're made to grow,
I'll follow your way,
And until then, I will ask you to enjoy the tides,
It's been a while, I'll see you on the other side.

~

Show me the way, you crooked guide,
Venturing like a shadow,
Through days and nights,
Crouching like a predator,
That has tasted blood once,
Turning the wisest of us deluded,
Nothing short of a dunce.

Watch me bloom into a garden,
From the seed you sow,
Transform me into a species that is courageous,
To live without having to know,
That is daring to stand on this ledge,
Where everything is supposed to be fair,
Yet the strongest of us continue to fetch.

Sliding through doors made of paper,
Burning through the haze of a rehearsed caricature,
Was it easy to find a difficult spot?
Or was it a tornado that led to another?

Give me a light,
For this magic flame,
Sizzle me a chapter,
Extinguishing any self-proclaimed fame.

Wrapped in its mist,
Elevated by its kiss,
A calmness injects itself through the streams,
Rubbing against every wound that chose to be caressed
by this steam.

~

The thing is, there is never a point in life when you'll be going through nothing. For that, you'd need to be lifeless, in other words dead, and I think that in itself is a big deal to be going through. So, take your pick.

AWAKENING

(i)

Awakening

Being afraid is the strongest act. It shows we had the courage to care.

~

Talk second,
First make that move,
Whisper what should be heard,
This game is to be played by two.

Look here,
There's nothing to be offered just yet,
Progress takes time,
There's no rush,
We're building a kingdom, not a shed.

~

The world was already made with everything
we needed,

Then we started finding what we wanted and that got
us to be greedy.

~

Forget the silhouettes of the past,
And the shadows that didn't last,
Open your eyes to the summer sky,
Sun rays burn fast,
As the rain begins to dry,
While you sit,
Holding the past,
Within a whiskey glass,
While you smile,
Holding back,
Tears for all that you lack,
So, forget the shadows of all that's gone,
And open up to all that's to come,
Follow the raindrops till the sun comes to your feet,
Stay awake and don't lose hope,
While you crumple those sheets,
Because all that you know is as inconsistent as that
summer glow,
And all that you'll ever see,
Can be with you for eternity.

~

I'm making life go by fast. Either it gets me away from you or towards you, but I'm going fast.

~

Everyone has a start-up. Each of ours is called life and they are the owners to the failures and more importantly the success that leads to this one-off creation we are blessed with.

~

In life we find ourselves forever choosing between left
and right,

Never questioning the what but always the why,

Continuously screaming about the what if, as if it
were bad,

Suggesting connotations of the end, and not the road
ahead,

The lines on our faces are credited to the frowns,

Smiles taken as momentary pleasures as we instantly let
sorrow make us drown,

Sipping a cold one to numb the pain,
Forgetting we signed up for it,
Selfish to think there will only be gain,

But everything good doesn't come to an end,
It just stops at one point and chooses the left while you
go right,

It answers the what as you question the why,
Screams to whispers, it all subsides,

Finding a place within, where there was warmth,
Each shrapnel tucks itself fooling you to believe
it's gone,
But nothing good comes to an end.

~

And . . . Perhaps Love

Let me tell you a story,
Seeing that we just met,
This moment will come to a close,
It's up to us the time we set.

Come a little closer,
Not so close,
I'll whisper some flaws,
You find the pros.

Don't question the meet,
In fact, forget the questions for life,
Life is an intimidating word,
Depends on whether we choose for it to be smooth
Or sharp as a knife.

There is no pressure,
For how this pans out,
You say it in whispers,
Hoping I hear it as a shout.

You see me believing,
As more moments pass by,
You expect me to try?
That's the first recipe for a cry.

Let me listen to your story,
Do I play the villain?
Do I play a part at all?
Or am I played by the devil?

This can last forever,
Did that just make you take a step back?
Maybe it'll end in a minute,
Did that just make you stay on track?

There is a point,
You'll figure through this circle,
Let me tell you a secret,
We're all first-timers trying our luck.

~

Nothing like happiness.

Nothing like, happiness.

You'll experience both, and there's nothing wrong
in that.

Breathe, keep going and you'll conquer.

~

Call me infinity

Call me infinity,
I'm not here to stay,
I'm not here to stop,
Learning through each day.

Call me invisible,
I'm not here to stick,
I'm not here to fade,
Graduating to a new grade.

Call me insane,
That I will resonate,
That I will laugh to,
I won't change to any other way.

Call me immune,
From all these troubles,
They're not strangers,
But long-lost brothers.

Call me immeasurable,
There are no limits,
You gift me a new day,
I'll learn a new way,

To buy more time,
Never to sell, for a short shine,
This is no short run,
There is no short cut,
We aren't a day's play,
This isn't a day's game,
This is infinity,
Invisible insanity,
Growing through an immunity,
From each day's fall, and
Each second's rise.

~

Nothing in life is perfect. It's being able to deal with our imperfections that gets us closest to what we label perfection.

~

And . . . Perhaps Love

I'm searching for the right questions,
You can keep your answers,
I'm finding a mountain to climb.

There's a sandstorm that's passed,
A tornado looms in the corner,
You see the waves retract,
To cause a shiver to whatever remains intact.

I'm climbing up the ladder,
You can remove it when I'm up,
I'm not coming back down,
This is a one-way journey I've found.

Heat waves beat the cold,
Lifeless now, herculean now,
I am the captain of the flight,
Turned into the captain of the Titanic somehow.

Everything seems a little hazy,
Clarity has its own phases,
Walking in like an uncalled guest,
There are no answers, for this inconsistent test,
Yet I pass, as I examine myself,
There seems to be no cure,
For this never-ending fest.

~

Sanil Sachar

Don't hide away in emotions
Come settle within this commotion
The ins and outs of this open jail
Hail upon those who never settle to fail.

~

Let it flow,
It can be anything you want,
Let it go,
It can be anything that doesn't want you,
Be a boat,
Surfing through it all,
It is everything you've desired,
It is everything worth the fall,
Smile through it,
It is the pain testing your intentions,
It is the moment questioning your resistance,
It is here, embrace it as it evolves,
It is a beautiful life, what else do you want?

~

A breeze whisked past us,
Leaving a craving for this sensation,
A tickle of yesterday,
A tease of tomorrow,
A moment, a moment ago.

Did you smile when it introduced itself?
Did you smile when it passed?
Did you smile at all, my friend?
Because this breeze will pass.

A whisper kisses our ear,
No secrets being shared,
These are naked thoughts exploring themselves.

A song of yesterday,
A song of tomorrow,
A melody, melodious in its vulnerability.

Did you sing along when it followed?
Did you sing along when it paused?
Did you sing at all, my friend?
Because this song will reach its dramatic pause.

A ray glimmers on our faces,
Brightening up everything the eye can see,

And . . . Perhaps Love

A light of yesterday,
A light of tomorrow,
A beam, beaming through our darkness.

Did you see it when it turned on?
Did you see it when it faded?
Did you see it all, my friend?
Because this light was there to carry you on.

A fragrance sets itself within you,
Inhaling nostalgia and whiffs of terror,
An aroma, as aromatic as a freshly plucked flower.

Did you breathe in when it sprayed itself?
Did you breathe in when it passed?
Did you breathe in at all, my friend?
Because the nearest aroma is from the seeds you sow,
and all that it plants.

A tanginess sets home on your tongue,
Each bite bursting flavours from a light marked 'to be
done',
A taste of yesterday,
A taste of tomorrow,
A taste, as tasteful as your favourite delicacy,
Did you taste it when it was cooked?

Sanil Sachar

Did you taste it when it passed?
Did you taste it at all, my friend?
Feed that hunger,
This is here to stay; it will not pass.

~

At the start, we come in this world by the togetherness of love. It's this bond that gives us a start from a sapling to a branch. Through this, we make our own decisions and grow, some into trees and the others into smaller plants. But we all want to be a dense forest. Never alone because we're taught loneliness is the indication of the lack of love. Every decision is spurred by love. The perfect synonym to life.

~

Strings attached to the loose ends of a part,
That sways like a pendulum the moment a voice
embarks,
On an excursion of what could be,
There's a moment of madness in this therapy.

Let it flow,
Let it bleed,
A jugular vein impatient to be free,
A volcanic eruption raring to see,
The reaction to an inevitable act of destiny.

~

Do it.
Find a reason, a purpose, a goal.
A goal to stay patient for,
A purpose navigating you to this goal,
A reason, whatever it might be, wherever it might be,
whoever it might be,
Pushing you to endure any pain now, for tomorrow.
Do it.
Beat yourself, today.
Not later but today,
Do it, for tomorrow.
Everything you want is already with you,
It's up to you how long you want to keep it.
Do it.
All that you tell yourself you will,
Everything you dream of while you're asleep,
For everyone you see while you are awake,
Do it.
Do everything you love, and you will love everything
you do,
Do it because it will stay beyond you,
It will take you beyond measure,
It will make you not go through life but live it,
Do what you want tomorrow, today,

Because time will fly when you combine the reason,
the purpose, the goal,
All this, just so you can,
Do it.

~

You will succeed. You will fail. You will love. You will hate. But the bright side of this is that it is you who will do everything. And that is life and that is the bitter truth.

Float,
With no direction,
Sway,
With minimal introspection,
Host,
All the fears you hide from,
Befriend,
Each mistake that'll make you strong.

You're an example,
To no one but yourself,
You're a sample,
From everything you put on your shelf.

Breathe,
There is chaos in this peace,
Exhale,
Knowing you're the only one you should please.

~

We can all sit in the same place in the open. The sun will beam equally on our faces. There'll be no divide in how nature will treat us. These borders are only created by hands that will never be big enough to hold everything it wants.

~

Stillness, abused by erratic movements,
Patience, a devil by its side.

Amusement, lost with lost innocence,
Spontaneity, forgotten due to impulsive due diligence.

The past taught lessons,
No attendance monitored,
Teachings unheard,
The future presented a re-examination,
Unprepared, guided by exhilaration.

Silence, interrupted by silent thoughts,
Echoes, sung like a chorus as the mind's church bells
sleep to a constant white sound.

Anticipation, a lukewarm medicine for restless nights,
Expectation, a greed unsettled despite earning respite.

Embrace me with peace,
I'll dissect it to pieces,
Inspect it through a microscope of life's thesis.

Gift me chaos,
I'll caress it to sleep,

And . . . Perhaps Love

A cyclone is a mere gush of wind,
The hourglass empties itself,
At the end, is where I begin.

~

For all those who have left, I don't think I've lost them.
I've told myself I'll meet them in the next section.
The level I haven't yet been promoted to.

~

You.
I seek.
I can't hide.
I preach.
I can't guide.
I treat.
I can't imbibe.
I see.
I can't drive.
I breathe.
I can't survive.
I feel.
I am alive.

~

This is a happy story.
It's also a love story.
Which makes it sad.
So, this is a happy and a not-so-happy story.
This is about struggle.
It's about overcoming struggle.
This is life.

Acknowledgements

For every mistake I've made, they have seen the repercussions coming before and yet never interfered in the journey and what it led me to. They have never been judgemental, they've smiled with belief that the words will always flow at the end. For this, and for the courage they have infused me with, I'd like to thank Mom and Dad, Sita and Sanjiv Sachar. You are the closest I know to an external force on earth.

To my sister, Shreya, my first friend, who I had no choice but to make, and one she couldn't unfriend. Thank you for looking out for me. It is this comfort that enables me to confidently tread lines that get thinner, till they get comfortable to run on. Most importantly, I thank, bless and provide all my love to Rohan and you for bringing Aaria into our lives.

Acknowledgements

To Aaria, my gorgeous and comedic niece; the moment I first saw you, I forgot everything else in life, and it's this purity, joy and calmness you bring us from the moment we were blessed with you that makes everything more meaningful. Completing and reworking this book has been a breeze because it's hard not to enjoy life with you around. I'm the happiest naming you here, and I hope by the time you're allowed to read this, I would have written you your very own story.

Rishi Jolly, a man I can't wait for the world to hear sing, has been the receiver of texts, calls and studio sessions that led to a string of words that make these pages. Your brutal honesty instilled humility, after carving through each layer of irritation that made me realize: I need to seek the truth in order to write it.

There was a person who once told me, 'If you don't do this, who will miss out?' and the depth of those words lead me to search for 'this' in everything I am thankful of contributing my time to. Writing for me is therefore not a medium of art, but a replacement of each breath that makes up my life. I owe my sanity and insanity to writing.

Before I come to a close, these words are for you, and I know as you flip through the pages, you'll know where you find yourself.